# 30 SECRETS
## FROM A 6 FIGURE
## ONLINE ENTREPRENEUR

## AFTER 2 YEARS IN BUSINESS & 300K+ REVENUE...

**MATEEN.S**

**Bonus!** - As a way of saying thanks, here's a short book that is guaranteed to excel your business career. It helped me greatly and will do the same for you if you can internalise the concepts.

**Download Here** → *http://goo.gl/iYx5aC*

## Join Our Insider List

Get Our Premium Books Below for Only 99 Cents!

Join Here ^  http://goo.gl/wcNCvW

*Insiders get Discounts to our Upcoming Book Titles upon Book Launch.*

<u>COMING SOON</u>

# 30 SECRETS FROM A 6 FIGURE ENTREPRENEUR

## After 3 Years In Business and 300k+ Revenue

Written By:

Mateen Soudagar

Brought to you by AffEngineer.com

www.AffEngineer.com Copyright © 2015 by AffEngineer Publishing

## Disclaimer

# Table of Contents

# Introduction

Entrepreneurship isn't easy. Often it's a longer than expected, gruelling road to success.
Three years ago, when I quit my day job to give entrepreneurship my full-time focus, I was confident I'd make it but I had no clue it would take me a whole year to start earning money.

My mindset now has changed drastically since I first started. I benefitted greatly from people that I would admire and read about. Personal stories, videos, even small tweets, anything that would give me insight as to how an entrepreneur thinks.

Below I'll go through 25 points of difference between the me 3 years ago and the me now. I hope you enjoy reading this book as much as I enjoyed writing it.

## About Me

I started my first day of full-time entrepreneurship in November 2012. Prior to that I worked as a Graduate Civil Engineer in a Construction firm in Australia.

I've always been interested in business. At school I'd buy and sell USB's and other gadgets that would make me small profits. At University I did the same with PS3's, Phones, Games, Other gaming consoles, laptops, basically anything I could get my hands on. It was the thrill of creating wealth from nothing that excited me. Profit was cool but I had a great part time job that would pay more then my uni expenses so I didn't really need to do this. I just did it as a hobby and to experiment with the business world.

It was no surprise that when I started full time work, it didn't excite me anywhere near as much as the business world did. It's not that the work activities were boring. Being unable to put my business mind to work when I'd spot opportunities is what would frustrate me.

2 Years into my career in a very healthy corporate

firm with a lot of potential to grow, to everyone's shock and horror, I put in my resignation. I had saved up 80% of my income which would give me around 2 years to start making money and was ready to dive back into what I loved doing. This time, full-time.

It's been 3 years since that day and I've tried a variety of different business ideas. From buying and selling things on eBay/Alibaba to flipping cars to making phone apps and websites. With each endeavour I learned what I liked and what I didn't and eventually made my money with Internet Marketing.

# 30 Insights

## 1. Thinking You'll do all the Work you Schedule Yourself to do

In the lead up month to quitting work, I couldn't think of anything other than what I was going to do with all the spare time I'll now have. I'd jot down schedules and plans of how I was going to live my life, where I'd spend most of my time, long term goals and short term goals, I think I refined my schedule at least 50 different times.

A sample day would look like,

5:00am wake up & go for jog
5:30am watch some documentaries on history/politics & educate self on the world
7:00am start work
1:00pm eat lunch
2:00pm start second work shift
5:00pm finish work
6:00pm boxing training
8:00pm make food/preparation
10:00pm sleep

Looks pretty productive doesn't it? Well it is...if you can do it.

I thought working for yourself would be like school. You could allocate certain times of the day to certain 'subjects' and work on them everyday. For most full-time entrepreneurs including myself, this is far from the truth.

When you begin working for yourself, all your body wants to do is everything it was deprived of doing while working full-time. From playing games to just sleeping in. Sure, you'll be motivated for a while because you're eager to begin working on your business plan but no way will you be able to jump straight into a consistent schedule.

In fact, I'm 2 years in and still struggling to maintain a work schedule. I'll have solid 4 hour work days for a week followed by just 4 hours of work in that one full week. It depends on the work I get and how much I want to relax and do nothing.

At the start, give yourself some time to adjust to this new change. Working for yourself is a whole different beast compared to working for someone else. You have NO pressure to do the work apart from your own drive.

Space yourself out so you start to fix into something regularly. Don't get frustrated, schedules and habits are picked up and perfected along the journey. Successful entrepreneurs who work hard consistently do so because they've been working at their habits for years. Don't expect to follow them perfectly straight away. Respect the process and you won't be dissapointed.

## 2. Saturated vs Unsaturated Mentality

In the business world, you'll hear the word 'saturation' a lot. For those of you who don't know what that means, it's basically a way of saying, 'there's no more opportunities to make money in that industry anymore'.

Saturation is a scientific term indicating that something is full. In entrepreneurship it's often used by lazy people to rule out an opportunity.

When I first started online marketing, I picked a few, common products that pretty much everyone would have promoted at some point. I went with the most obvious marketing method which most people would have ruled out thinking it's too obvious and someone would already be on to it. Wrong. There was almost no competition for it and I ended up making $100-$300/day profit for a a good 6 months.

If I had passed it off as being too obvious I wouldn't have given it a shot. That income stream helped me get through my early years of entrepreneurship.

Even now, I'll come across some ideas/niches that I now people have been hammering at since the early days of the internet but I'll STILL give it a shot. *You never know until you try*. Don't give up on anything until you try it no matter how silly the idea might seem to someone else.

### 3. Competition is a GOOD Thing

Yep, you read that right. For a LONG LONG time I would think of an idea, then google if 'the idea has already been taken', then ditch the idea because 99% of the time it 'HAS been taken'.

I'm sure you've heard it many times where you'd bring up an idea in front of friends and family and someone in the group would state that the 'idea has already been taken'.

I don't know how many ideas I discarded this way and for a long time I thought it was the right thing to do. That's until I heard Mark Cuban say that competition is a GOOD thing and the more people trying to fight for a piece of the pie, the more money there is to be made.

Things started to make a lot of sense after I heard that.

Why are all the food places in shopping centre all placed right next to each other? What if Burger King didn't open a branch in a particular place because Mcdonalds was too close.

In most food courts here in Australia, where there's a Mcdonalds, there's a KFC & Hungry Jacks near by. They're all fighting for a piece of the food industry which is big enough to accommodate them all.

From now on, I don't even worry about competition. No more seeing if certain keywords have too high of a competition to include in my blog posts. I now look for popular topics, popular apps, popular business ideas that give insight into how hungry a market is.

The more competition, the better. If you believe in your ability and can outwork the competition, it's always worth a shot.

I'm not saying to make the next FaceBook but I AM saying to take note of what FaceBook users like, (social sharing and interacting with each other), and try build something else similar to it. This is how companies like Pinterest, Instagram, Snapchat were born.

Bottom line, don't worry about competition. Worry about making a killer product and getting killer sales or amassing an active user base. At the end of the day, this is what matters.

## 4. Business isn't Easy

I'm not sure if 'easy' is the right word but a LOT of people, including myself underestimate the effort and patience needed to build a _consistently profitable_ business. One that you can live off comfortably or even one that gives you some healthy part-time income. Sure you can make a few hundred dollars here and there but something that is growing and expanding while being profitable is hard to create.

It takes a lot of patience and perseverance to break through. These words may not be foreign to you but the extent of them IS something you would rarely encounter.

November 2012, I had quit work, had some savings in the bank and was ready to dive into entrepreneurship activities. There was nothing specific in mind but I had a list of ideas I was itching to get through.

So I did. One by one, I did them, re-evaluated, did another, repeated. After 6 months of trying at least 20 different ideas I came across internet marketing. People making up to 5 figures profit a day! It was mind boggling and I just wanted to be part of the action.

It's different when you're working on an idea you KNOW works. The 20 or so things I tried before were little experiments. I began thinking, maybe it's better to just try emulate an already proven business idea out there. It obviously works for someone else, why shouldn't it work for me?

With this new mindset I started reading like a mad man. I listed all the resources I found handy on my blog which you can check out any time.

I'd read income reports of others making small fortunes on the internet almost everyday which kept me motivated. I started dabbling in FaceBook marketing, Google marketing, learning how to make websites, reading forums and articles, anything I could get my hands on that would give me some sort of insight in internet marketing.

I remember 3 weeks in, I was spending $5 - $80/day and seeing no results back. I was becoming demotivated. At the start it was easy to work 10 hour days, but 3 weeks later when your still seeing no results, you need to pull motivation from somewhere. THIS is where persistence and patience really kick in. This is the part where you need to switch your body in robot mode and just work through it. Force your body to keep typing, keep reading, keep making things happen.

A day after the 3$^{rd}$ week I made my first few sales. I was still $2 in the red for the day but seeing money come through was validation that this internet marketing thing really works!

A week after that I had my first profitbale day. It took another 2 months after that to start making money consistently and finally be confident in my own ability to make money in internet marketing. Below is a spreadsheet I used to keep track of my first few months.

| | DATE | TOTAL COST | TOTAL REVENUE | TOTAL P/L | ROI % |
|---|---|---|---|---|---|
| | 21/7/2013 | $3.70 | $0.00 | -$3.70 | -100.00% |
| | 22/7/2013 | $10.00 | $0.00 | -$10.00 | -100.00% |
| | 23/7/2013 | $6.36 | $0.00 | -$6.36 | -100.00% |
| | 24/7/2013 | $4.93 | $0.00 | -$4.93 | -100.00% |
| | 25/7/2013 | $4.59 | $0.00 | -$4.59 | -100.00% |
| | 26/7/2013 | $2.89 | $0.00 | -$2.89 | -100.00% |
| | 27/7/2013 | $7.42 | $0.00 | -$7.42 | -100.00% |
| | 28/7/2013 | $56.60 | $0.00 | -$56.60 | -100.00% |
| | 29/7/2013 | $27.08 | $0.00 | -$27.08 | -100.00% |
| | 30/7/2013 | $65.52 | $0.00 | -$65.52 | -100.00% |
| July | 31/7/2013 | $79.13 | $0.00 | -$79.13 | -100.00% |
| | 1/8/2013 | $31.45 | $0.00 | -$31.45 | -100.00% |
| | 2/8/2013 | $37.32 | $0.00 | -$37.32 | -100.00% |
| | 3/8/2013 | $27.65 | $0.00 | -$27.65 | -100.00% |
| | 4/8/2012 | $3.86 | $0.00 | -$3.86 | -100.00% |
| | 5/8/2013 | $0.00 | $0.00 | $0.00 | #DIV/0! |
| | 6/8/2013 | $0.00 | $0.00 | $0.00 | #DIV/0! |
| | 7/8/2013 | $0.00 | $0.00 | $0.00 | #DIV/0! |
| | 8/8/2013 | $0.00 | $0.00 | $0.00 | #DIV/0! |
| | 9/8/2013 | $0.07 | $0.00 | -$0.07 | -100.00% |
| | 10/8/2013 | $0.27 | $0.00 | -$0.27 | -100.00% |
| | 11/8/2013 | $0.70 | $0.00 | -$0.70 | -100.00% |
| | 12/8/2013 | $19.31 | $17.25 | -$2.06 | -10.67% |
| | 13/8/2013 | $28.17 | $11.50 | -$16.67 | -59.18% |
| | 14/8/2013 | $14.71 | $5.75 | -$8.96 | -60.91% |
| | 15/8/2013 | $12.02 | $0.00 | -$12.02 | -100.00% |
| | 16/8/2013 | $15.81 | $11.50 | -$4.31 | -27.26% |
| | 17/8/2013 | $16.78 | $5.75 | -$11.03 | -65.73% |
| | 18/8/2013 | $18.03 | $45.54 | $27.51 | 152.58% |
| | 19/8/2013 | $59.11 | $46.00 | -$13.11 | -22.18% |
| | 20/8/2013 | $40.46 | $37.50 | -$2.96 | -7.32% |
| | 21/8/2013 | $35.08 | $50.00 | $14.92 | 42.53% |
| | 22/8/2013 | $47.22 | $31.25 | -$15.97 | -33.82% |
| | 23/8/2013 | $49.62 | $50.00 | $0.38 | 0.77% |
| | 24/8/2013 | $49.61 | $50.00 | $0.39 | 0.79% |
| | 25/8/2013 | $61.93 | $50.00 | -$11.93 | -19.26% |
| | 26/8/2013 | $63.27 | $37.50 | -$25.77 | -40.73% |
| | 27/8/2013 | $84.47 | $81.74 | -$2.73 | -3.23% |
| | 28/8/2013 | $73.75 | $75.00 | $1.25 | 1.69% |
| | 29/8/2013 | $61.57 | $25.00 | -$36.57 | -59.40% |
| | 30/8/2013 | $60.03 | $31.25 | -$28.78 | -47.94% |
| August | 31/8/2013 | $38.30 | $25.00 | -$13.30 | -34.73% |

| | Date | | | | |
|---|---|---|---|---|---|
| | 1/9/2013 | $56.20 | $75.00 | $18.80 | 33.45% |
| | 2/9/2013 | $54.38 | $37.50 | -$16.88 | -31.04% |
| | 3/9/2013 | $103.38 | $88.00 | -$15.38 | -14.88% |
| | 4/9/2013 | $69.12 | $43.70 | -$25.42 | -36.78% |
| | 5/9/2013 | $109.86 | $72.00 | -$37.86 | -34.46% |
| | 6/9/2013 | $95.46 | $60.09 | -$35.37 | -37.05% |
| | 7/9/2013 | $89.56 | $85.70 | -$3.86 | -4.31% |
| | 8/9/2013 | $66.34 | $64.10 | -$2.24 | -3.38% |
| | 9/9/2013 | $98.21 | $63.30 | -$34.91 | -35.55% |
| | 10/9/2013 | $147.38 | $80.20 | -$67.18 | -45.58% |
| | 11/9/2013 | $112.54 | $32.00 | -$80.54 | -71.57% |
| | 12/9/2013 | $98.74 | $48.80 | -$49.94 | -50.58% |
| | 13/9/2013 | $72.95 | $96.40 | $23.45 | 32.14% |
| | 14/9/2013 | $109.67 | $151.19 | $41.52 | 37.86% |
| | 15/9/2013 | $100.28 | $62.80 | -$37.48 | -37.37% |
| | 16/9/2013 | $75.85 | $45.60 | -$30.25 | -39.88% |
| | 17/9/2013 | $102.45 | $75.39 | -$27.06 | -26.41% |
| | 18/9/2013 | $136.80 | $185.20 | $48.40 | 35.38% |
| | 19/9/2013 | $154.46 | $219.79 | $65.33 | 42.30% |
| | 20/9/2013 | $132.42 | $106.80 | -$25.62 | -19.35% |
| | 21/9/2013 | $139.93 | $124.60 | -$15.33 | -10.96% |
| | 22/9/2013 | $115.03 | $174.20 | $59.17 | 51.44% |
| | 23/9/2013 | $160.26 | $141.50 | -$18.76 | -11.70% |
| | 24/9/2013 | $172.13 | $207.80 | $35.67 | 20.73% |
| | 25/9/2013 | $96.04 | $118.60 | $22.57 | 23.50% |
| | 26/9/2013 | $95.98 | $135.11 | $39.13 | 40.77% |
| | 27/9/2013 | $110.17 | $71.20 | -$38.97 | -35.37% |
| | 28/9/2013 | $98.14 | $124.60 | $26.46 | 26.96% |
| | 29/9/2013 | $121.47 | $129.40 | $7.93 | 6.52% |
| September | 30/9/2013 | $141.99 | $162.90 | $20.91 | 14.73% |
| | 1/10/2013 | $120.09 | $77.20 | -$42.89 | -35.71% |
| | 2/10/2013 | $150.29 | $89.80 | -$60.49 | -40.25% |
| | 3/10/2013 | $103.69 | $95.80 | -$7.89 | -7.60% |
| | 4/10/2013 | $166.27 | $88.44 | -$77.83 | -46.81% |
| | 5/10/2013 | $125.90 | $78.40 | -$47.50 | -37.73% |
| | 6/10/0203 | $33.24 | $27.40 | -$5.84 | -17.57% |
| | 7/10/2013 | $62.51 | $29.00 | -$33.51 | -53.61% |
| | 8/10/2013 | $60.60 | $47.00 | -$13.60 | -22.44% |
| | 9/10/2013 | $40.90 | $41.00 | $0.10 | 0.24% |
| | 10/10/2013 | $74.51 | $81.95 | $7.44 | 9.99% |
| | 11/10/2013 | $88.49 | $122.10 | $33.61 | 37.98% |
| | 12/10/2013 | $115.31 | $110.35 | -$4.96 | -4.30% |
| | 13/10/2013 | $106.87 | $102.75 | -$4.12 | -3.86% |
| | 14/10/2013 | $82.55 | $122.75 | $40.20 | 48.70% |
| | 15/10/2013 | $98.58 | $64.20 | -$34.38 | -34.88% |
| | 16/10/2013 | $89.77 | $198.37 | $108.60 | 120.98% |
| | 17/10/2013 | $93.98 | $254.00 | $160.02 | 170.27% |
| | 18/10/2013 | $106.47 | $164.40 | $57.93 | 54.41% |
| | 19/10/2013 | $116.63 | $188.40 | $71.77 | 61.54% |
| | 20/10/2013 | $128.41 | $262.25 | $133.84 | 104.23% |
| | 21/10/2013 | $118.11 | $333.20 | $215.09 | 182.11% |
| October | 22/10/2013 | $122.48 | $330.40 | $207.92 | 169.76% |
| | | **$6,661.61** | **$6,680.16** | $18.55 | **0.28%** |

You see all that red? Those were all negative days. Days, I'd put in 8-10 hours of work but end on a loss. I had to just keep pushing forward if I wanted to make this work and I knew as long as I'm learning I'm getting closer to my goal.

At the end of it, I spent 6.5k until I broke even and rest all is history.

This endeavour taught me how to switch to robot mode when you need to get things done. Motivation is something that comes and goes. You need to be able to bring it out from somewhere when it's gone and STILL output the same work efficiency towards your business.

Every entrepreneur has had to conquer this at some stage so you will need to as well.

## 5. Detaching self to Money

This is related to the above point.

Most people that want to create wealth from having their business are very hesitant to spend money. I don't blame them. Everything is new and it's hard to figure out where money is best spent.

At some point you realise that the only way to make REAL money is to spend money. I'm not saying put down $1,000 on a professional design of your logo. But I AM saying to spend $100/year on having a nice website up and running for your business so people know what service/product you offer.

Spend money to learn, on coaches, on seminars, (as long as they're affordable).

As you spend money, you being learning that money is traded for information in the business world. Information that gives you a better fighting chance at your business. Not every expenditure will have a direct effect towards increasing your revenue. Sometimes you'll spend $200 to test if a certain marketing technique works. If you find out it doesn't, that's great, at least now you know it doesn't work.

Eventually you'll become detached to money which is a good thing as long as you're still smart about it. Again, don't be spending big money on items that don't really need it at this stage of your business. At the start of your business you need to be spending money on validation, testing your product/service, bringing traffic to your website/shop and seeing how people react. Is there interest or isn't there? The last thing you want to do is work on an idea for months, (sometimes even years!), only to put it out there and realise no one wants it. This is all stuff you need to figure out asap.

Any working business knows how to spend money to make his or hers business better. Eventually you will need to learn this. Start spending small. Fiverr.com is a great little website where you can outsource small activities for $5. You'll learn how to trade $$ for effort and train the mind to think value over money.

## 6. Treating Business as a Full-Time Job

Almost everyone I know wants to make a part-time income that supplements their full-time job. I mean, who wouldn't want a few hundred dollars extra every month? A few hundred would go a long way in paying the bills.

The problem with this mentality is it makes business seem like a 'part-time' thing. Something that you can work on a few hours a week and still make money from it.

Well, it can be done BUT there is no business I know, part-time OR full-time that hasn't started with people putting a lot work and effort at the start. Sure, you can get to a stage that you have to work a few hours a week to keep it running but don't expect to be doing that straight away and seeing results.

My own blog took 100s of hours of writing, making youtube videos, marketing, etc to get up and running and earning money. It took a good year for it to start earning me a decent income and although now that it can finally be worked on for just a few hours a week, I still need to be consistent with my work or my income will begin to drop.

If you want to have any sort of business at some stage of your life, be prepared to give it a huge focus at the start. None of this, "I'll work on it in my spare time" thing. Make it a priority. Work on it everyday after work for 3-4 hours. It takes many hours to learn the fundamentals and to generally get through the learning phase so it's best to get through this phase as quick as possible.

Do this consistently for a few months and you should start seeing results.

Bottom line? Give your business the respect it deserves. If you don't prioritise it, it won't grow or bare fruit. It's like giving water to your plants once every fortnight. It might keep them alive, (barely), but it won't be enough to make it grow into something healthy.

## 7. Worrying About What People Think

The business world is stressful as it is. On top of that you need to be able to deal with naysayers and people who are generally interested in your defeat.

People don't believe in themselves and at some stage of their life have just excepted that the business world is a utopia created for a certain group of people that are destined to have it. For the majority of others, it's just a dream. Something you're not 'good at'.

Well, NO ONE is 'good at' business at the start. How would they be? How would they know how to sell something if they've never done it before? Humans are creatures that learn through experience and unless they've had the chance to go through that experience they'll never learn.

Business is the same way, throw yourself in and start absorbing experience. Any experience is good and it will continually shape you to be a better business person. Not many people understand this and many of them will say words that might put you down.

When I first started my business, I'd tell people, excitedly that I made a whole $5 today. For me, it was a huge achievement, to be able to generate money on your own without the need for an 'employer'. For others it was a funny story. Some guy left his job to make $5 a day. If I had been disheartened by all this and let it get to me, I would have gone back to work but I knew these people are different. They don't know what I know.

I didn't worry about all this. They're not me. I am me. And I am different to all them. We're a small minority of people that believe in our ability. We may be a little delusional sometimes but this is necessary to evolve into the person that make it a reality.

The majority of successful people in the world started from humble beginnings. From entrepreneurs to musicians, they kept working at their art till they got so good, the world paid them back. If they gave up at the start because some moron came along and told them they're not good enough, where would they be?

Business is something anyone can do as long as

they realise the above. Always stay positive and keep telling yourself that things will work out. Be smart about the time you put in. The more the better. Be smart about the activities and people you surround yourself with. Try become part of a forum, a skype group, a collection of people with similar minds who have similar interests.

The more you surround yourself with people that wish for your betterment and understand where you want to go, the better chance at success you're going to give yourself.

## 8. Having a Healthy Savings

I've read too many stories about people starting
from nothing. It's great and very motivational.
Many successful and famous entrepreneurs were
living out of their car at some point, desperate to
make things work.

I take these stories as inspiration but personally,
I'd never want to be put in these situations. I have
a family to take care of and be there for and at
certain times will have to decide on being there
for them over making my business work.
With this type of mind, I always recommend
people to have a healthy savings before they start.
I had around 50k in the bank before I started.
Enough to keep me going for 2 years of moderate
expenditures.

This kept me thinking straight and focussed on
my business. The last thing you want is to have
all these ideas you want to implement but no
money to do it. If this is you, I would recommend
to save a good amount of money before you dive
in. An amount that will give you the freedom and
mental clarity to focus. I've known people for
years who've had the right business mind but have

always been in debt. Unable to spend and always trying to borrow more money. They just don't get it.

If you don't know how to save, you will never be able to grow a business to a point of profitability. A healthy business needs a well managed cash flow and if you can't manage your own cash flow, what makes you think you can manage one that's 10 x more complicated?

Start saving right now, it will go a long way in teaching you the mental discipline to spend wisely.

## 9. Financial Insecurity

Sometimes people that are so used to saving, have a hard time watching their account deplete with no signs of replenishment. This was me for a long time. Although I had 50k in the bank, watching it slowly get lesser and lesser with no revenue was making me financially insecure.

I had an inner scared voice constantly saying things like,
"you better go back to work or you'll lose everything"
"what if you lose it all and end up on the street?"
"You're wasting your time, a job will solve this problem"
"You're getting further and further away from your goal"

I never realised how powerful these voices would be. Every day I would have to deal with this feeling of insecurity. That I'll never get to where I want to be.

It's something I think everyone will have to deal with. Whatever the case, it's still better than being locked up in a job like a bird in a cage.

These are all challenges at the start of your business career to separate between those who really deserve it and those who are just dreamers. Conquer these voices by reminding yourself WHY you are doing it all and that everyone who made it, went through the same thing.

Even when you have a stable business, you'll find this feeling will still be there. You'll be worried about your business suddenly turning to dust, your niche becoming saturated, competition becoming a threat, the worries are endless. You need to be able to train the mind to keep looking forward. Trust in your ability to create wealth. As long as you have knowledge and experience, no one can take anything away from you.

## 10. Validation

Validation is a concept you hardly hear about. It's also something that takes a lot of time to train the mind to do.

Just like how in boxing, you need to reprogram your mind to react differently then you normally would when punches come your way, validation is something that the mind isn't programmed to do at the start.
Validation is the concept of 'testing your idea before spending time and effort to build it'.

The most intimidating phase of any business is to put it to the test. Bring some traffic to the product/service and see if anyone is interested enough to pull out their credit card and buy it. It's the part where you realise whether or not this wonderful idea of yours is just as wonderful in the eyes of your market.

Most people go about things the opposite way. They'll work on an idea for weeks, months, years, perfecting the design, the product, the concept, the website, etc. They mostly find excuses to work on something else to delay putting it out there. Whether they realise this or not, it IS what's happening.

By validating your idea, you're saving yourself a LOT of time. Validation can be in the form of setting up a simple website page that tells people to 'opt-in' for a special launch offer of your product. The more people that opt-in, obviously, the better the idea is.

If you spend $50 and 50 people opt-in, it's obviously a better idea then one with the same spend but only 5 people opting in.

Try even going one step further and getting people to actually put a deposit down.

The smart entrepreneur will sell his product before he builds it. It's better to get a huge list of _payed_ customers before production. This way you're guaranteed to make money.

Again, it takes a while to drill this type of mentality in but it's what differentiates great business men to the average.

Many people have seen Will Smiths movie, 'pursuit of happiness'. The movie starts off with

Will trying to sell portable bone-density scanners to doctors. He's spent his entire life savings in them which obviously makes him desperate to sell them.

Most likely he bought them in bulk thinking it was a good deal and that he would be able to make a profit if he could sell it all. After all, simple math usually leads to thinking you can turn a profit off bulk buys.

The problem with these is that hardly do they ALL sell. What if Will had told the person he was going to buy it off that he needs a few days to think about it. In those few days he called up 200+ medical firms and pitched them the idea of these machines and what they are capable of. He would have been able to gauge what the interest levels would be.

He could have bought a small sample, maybe 3 of them and tried to sell them. If they sold and the interest levels of these medical firms were high, he would have been in a much better position then not knowing the market at all. Even if, through calling people, he realises there's almost no interest, then he'd STILL be in a better position. He could have said no and tried to find another opportunity.

This is what validation is all about and it's slightly different for each idea. It's crucial to implement at the early stages of your business and should never be skipped. Your time is your most important commodity. Something that you have to think carefully before you spend. Don't worry about money. Money comes and goes, time doesn't.

Set a $/hr rate on yourself. Work this out when you start making money so you know how much your time is worth. If you're time is worth $50/hr then any task that can be outsourced for under that, outsource it.

## 11. Giving an Idea Enough Time vs Jumping Around

This point relates to the one above. You don't want to be giving up on an idea too early. In fact, many great ideas have been killed this way. Back when I never used to validate my ideas, I'd work on an idea for a week, then switch to something else. I'd work on that idea for another week and again, switch to something else that made me more excited then the first.

This process never ends. You're mind is a data bank of ideas and will keep giving you something almost every day.

Whether in validation mode, or post-validation mode, you need to give a certain amount of time to the idea before you move to something else.

If in validation mode, don't just call up 5 companies to try sell your product. Call up 100. Don't just drive 30 people to your website and see if anyone converts to a sale. Drive 1,000.

Accurate conclusions and findings about your business can only be obtained with a good amount of data accumulation. I'll get people emailing me saying they've spent $5 driving traffic to their website and no one bought anything or even opted in. Really? $5? Sometimes, I spend over $1,000 testing things to see what information I can learn about my idea.

I'm not telling you to spend months on your idea but don't keep jumping around like a frog to another juicy idea just because you're bored of your first idea. If you've tested the business and it gives you crappy feedback, that's a better reason to move on but if you're just moving on because your bored, you need to think about it more.

## 12. Business Skills are Transferrable

The best thing about business is that, no matter what you do, you'll always be learning something valuable. Business skills are learned everywhere and anywhere in business as long as you're applying yourself in it.

Whether you'r working on an offline business or an online one. Whether it's a take away shop or a blog, the concept of bringing customers, providing them value and keeping your business ticking is a process all businesses must aim to perfect.

At the start of your business journey, you may find yourself stuck. Not because you have no ideas, it's more because you have too may to chose from and you don't know where to begin! This happens to everyone and it has a term in the business world. It's called 'Paralysis by Analysis'. When you've read so much material that you're able to come up with ideas on the fly, you begin to bottle-neck with ideas and just don't know which one to focus on.

Just pick something and go for it. Write them

down in order of which you'd like to work on first. Don't move to the next idea until you've given this at least 2-3 months after a successful validation. You're never wasting your time since, even if this fails, the skills you'll learn from it will give your next venture a better fighting chance.

For the 6 months I was jumping from idea to idea like a no mad, trying websites, selling things on eBay, designing phone apps, I learned a lot of basic skills that kept making the next idea a lot easier to implement. When it all came together I made a boat load of money.
After this experience, I always feel, as long as your applying yourself to something in the business world, you're hardly ever wasting time, (unless you keep the same thing over and over again, never learning that you need to try something different to make it work).

## 13. First Idea Will Usually Not Work

I hate to be mr negative but this is mostly the case for the majority of first ideas. Almost every successful entrepreneur you hear about has a list of failed ideas behind him. Failure is normal, especially with your first endeavour.

I'm not telling you to go into your first idea thinking it will surely fail. Go into it thinking you'll make it work BUT don't be disheartened and shocked if it didn't turn out the way you wanted it to work.

It's like sitting an exam for the first time with no knowledge of the subject and expecting to pass. Maybe, if you're lucky, depending on the questions and your ability, you might pass but most people would fail.

What if you had done a few practice exams first? Would you have a better chance at success? What if you do 10 practice exams? What if you do 50? Would you ace the exam? Probably!

This is the same in the business world. Each business venture is a 'practice exam'. Something you learn off that gives your next idea a better chance. Keep doing this over and over again till you make it work.

A lot of people give up after their business dreams are 'shattered', from the failure of their business idea. They may have been brewing over the idea for months, years even, only to put it out there and realise no one's interested. People go back to work or decide that 'the business world is not for me'. Of course it's not for you...YET. But it will be for you if you continue what you're doing. In fact, you'll be a master of it eventually.

This is the difference in mind set successful people have. They know that as long as they keep going, they'll get what they want. The moment they give up, they lose so never give up with business.

## 14. Newest Programs & Technology Aren't Necessary

I know people that keep downloading the latest new software that's meant to 'increase your productivity' or 'organise you better'. It's good to experiment these things from time to time but if you have a working process that's efficient and gets the job done, 99% of the time you should be sticking to this process.

I still use notepad to list ideas, write down information, make a 'to-do' list etc. It's quick and easy to boot up. I know many people use ever note and swear by it but for me, I feel I don't need it.

Any images or websites I come across, I'll print screen on my phone.

I use excel to make simple tables to calculate profit/loss. The more simple things are, the easier it is for me.

You can always get things done without certain tools and products. Sure, they may increase productivity and general efficiency that little bit or maybe even make it worse, but most of the time, when you find something that works, stick to it.

## 15. Hoarding Information

I used to do this until I banned myself from it. That's right, it's so bad that I had to ban myself from it!

Having terabytes worth of tutorial videos to 100s of business ideas means nothing if you can't focus on even one. It's like having a library of books but not having the patience to go through a whole book before starting another.

You can read as much material as you want, but you'll still have to put in the work to get the results in the video.

Instead of knowing 50 different ways to make money, it's better to just know 1 and become the master at it.

When I first started, I had it in my head to learn every marketing platform there is out there. From SEO to FaceBook Marketing to Google to Intext & PPV, the list of marketing methods was endless. I'd jump from traffic source to traffic source trying to perfect each one. I was learning each day but my rate of learning was so slow it was almost unnoticeable.

I decided to ditch everything and become the master at one. That's when my results changed. Every time I've been focused on _just one_ goal, I've been able to achieve it. Even if I add a single goal more, the split focus will confuse my brain.

Most people that make a lot of money in the internet marketing do so in one thing. Instead of trying to be the jack of all trades, they become a sage in one trade and mine it for all it's worth. This is the right way to do things. Once you've capped the industry, (Highly unlikely), you can try something else but in terms of making money, don't hoard information, find something that works and keep working at it till you blow it out of the sky.

## 16. Action vs Inaction

This point is related to the above point. Reading is easy, anyone can do it. You're not someone different just because you know a little more about entrepreneurship then someone else. Just because you know how Steve Jobs was able to get his first contract or how Microsoft became Microsoft doesn't make you a better entrepreneur than anyone.

The ONLY thing that makes you a better entrepreneur is putting your knowledge to the test and immersing yourself in activities that force you to learn.

There's a lot of hesitation at the start and I understand that. Which idea should you go for? What if you're working on the wrong things? That's the thing about business, there is no wrong or right path. All paths lead to becoming a better business person and once you reach the tipping point where everything just clicks, you'll find that making money comes more easier.

Learning to swim is a great analogy. For a long time I was scared of the water. I've had a few near drowning experiences when I was young, couple that with watching jaws and you can understand why I stayed away from it.

I decided to confront this one day and booked a trip with some friends to go dive in the Great Barrier Reef - Queensland. It's a bit much to go from not knowing how to swim to diving the Great Barrier Reef but I had to force myself. The whole trip there I had nerves and at the moment I had to jump in to the water, I was staring at the ocean for a good $10 - 20$ seconds. I had a life jacket on, trained professionals around me and everything was safe. It was just me and my scared mind.

This is where, the only way to learn was to jump in. I'd force myself to learn it. That's exactly what happened. I jumped in and the life jacket kept me afloat. After at least 10 tries I learned how to breathe into the diving tank through the mouth piece and 20 minutes later I was exploring the bottom of the ocean with 2 of my best mates.

Business is just as intimidating to some people. There's so many things that can go wrong and if you're a very risk averse person, you'll feel very uncomfortable with this fact. You HAVE to learn to be comfortable with risks. Things will go wrong, way more often then they'll go wrong but you'll get better at it as long as you're in it.

## 17. Thinking Big but Acting Consistantly

With successful entrepreneurs promoting entrepreneurship through their seminars, everyone's becoming highly motivated to want to achieve great things. There's nothing wrong with this BUT it can be detrimental to the mentality of the beginner entrepreneur.

It's great to think big. You need to know where you want to be and it keeps you motivated, I get that. But in the process, don't forget that you STILL need to do all the small, supposedly boring tasks to get there. You'll still need to watch youtube tutorials on making websites or having hour long skype conversations with potential employees. You might have to spend hours cold-calling potential customers or even spend hours working in your smelly room learning HTML for the first time.

No matter how big you want to get, you'll still have to do the small tasks that matter. It's the accumulation of all these tasks and skills that bring you closer to the goal. At some point you'll have to 'find love for the little things'. You'll have to learn to do them. Whether you operate better listening to music or at a library where it's quiet, find your sweet spot.

The more you do these tasks, the better you'll get at them. Once you reach a proficiency level where you're quicker then most people at it and it becomes effortless, you'll begin to enjoy it.

Bottom line, think big, but still give importance to the small things that matter.

## 18. Sales/Feedback are Everything

There are countless tasks you can immerse yourself in that fall under the umbrella of entrepreneurship.

The most gruelling of them all is sales.

Sales are the corner stone of business. I've seen Kevin O'Leary from Shark Tanks say that the first thing he looks at when buying into a company is the sales division. At the end of the day, a business is in it to make money. Money for yourself. Money for your investors.

It's not an evil way to look at it. We need money to live, to pay for our food, shelter, education and everything in between so why shouldn't it?

People spend a lot of time delaying this part of the equation and it's one of the main reason businesses fail. Whether, it's a small business idea you started by yourself in your garage or something huge started by 10 people, sales/monetisation is one of the first things you need to look into. Any local service can be successful if you have the ability to just pick up the phone and start cold-calling or go door-knocking in your local neighbourhood. Most people don't want to do this and end up limiting their growth and revenue potential.

Good businesses understand the value of sales. There are some salesmen out there that earn more than top level CEO's. People in my industry, internet marketing, which is basically commission based selling in the online world, can earn up to 7 figures a month! It sounds mind boggling but it's true.

Before making tonnes of website posts, ebooks, paying $10,000 for a phone app, pouring money into the creation of a product, you need to figure out how this endeavour is going to make you money. Not only HOW but _'how much'_. Try nut it down to a figure you can aim for. Eg, for a phone app goal,

100,000 downloads of your app
40 - 50,000 active daily users
3 page visits/user
0.5% CTR on ads
120 – 150,000 page visits/day
600 – 750 ad clicks/day
~ $0.20 per ad click revenue

= $120-$150/day in advertising

The above numeric goals tell me exactly what I'm aiming for.

It's great to have an idea but if you can't think of a clear path for it to make you money then chances are, it won't. Sure, someone can buy you out if you get big enough but that hardly happens and if it does, the company making the purchase will have to see a way your business can make them money.

## 19. Difference Between Important Tasks and Non Important Tasks

Similar to the above point, there are a variety of tasks you can be doing at any given time, how do you know what to prioritise?

Over time, I've realised that there are two categories business activities normally fall under. activities that *directly contribute* to getting sales/feedback, (hard tasks), and activities that can be done at any time and *don't directly contribute* to sales/feedback, (soft tasks).

Examples of hard tasks

- Paying for FaceBook Ads and driving traffic to your sales page
- Contacting Instagram admins and seeing if they could post a pic of your product
- Pitching your idea to investors
- Putting your idea out on a reddit subforum for feedback

Examples of soft tasks

- Making your website/app look pretty
- Writing Posts/articles
- Buying bulk products
- Researching your competition
- Reading/brainstorming ideas

Notice the difference? Hard tasks involve facing the real world and letting it tell you whether your product is good or bad. Whether people are interested in pulling out their hard earned money and buying it or not. It's what will make or break you and is what you need to confront in order to make money.

Soft tasks, although important, can be done mostly, anytime. I can't tell you how many people I know who have bought products in bulk thinking it's a good deal then try and sell them slowly on gumtree and ebay. Why not flip the process and advertise on gumree/ebay first. If you get sales/interest then buy, if not, try another product.

Soft tasks are comfortable, there's no risk in someone telling you your idea sucks and so pretty much anyone can do it. It's safe and makes you feel like you're doing something productive but you can end up wasting a LOT of time doing this.

There are so many entrepreneurs that come on Shark Tank with a product they've been working on for years. Products they've spent their life savings on. It might look like a great product but when they mention they've made almost no sales, you can see the instant where faces of the Sharks turn from interested to 'I pity you'.

Sales, as mentioned in the previous point are the corner stone of a business. Not only do they bring you money but they tell you whether a customer will return or not, whether he or she will recommend it to someone else, whether they're excited enough to post it on FaceBook/Instagram.

REAL, unbiased feedback, not from your parents/siblings/friends, is king. It makes you grow into the type of entrepreneur that gets results. This is why not everyone can be a successful entrepreneur because not everyone is willing to take real feedback and grow from their mistakes/decisions.

## 20. Doing the Same Thing Over and Over Again is Insanity

I know people who have been doing the SAME thing for years and still haven't learned that their business idea sucks!

They may be in a niche that just doesn't like to spend. You can't expect to sell huge amounts of ice cream in winter the same way you would find it difficult to sell Purses to men. Sure, you'll get some sales, enough to get you by but if you want to turn this into a million dollar idea, think long and hard whether it has the potential or not.

The same thing applies to making blogs or websites. I made at least 10-15 blogs before I decided to stick to my current one. It came to a point where they kept failing because of the same damn reason. Marketing and traffic. I'd spend hours just writing articles and not do much to get them out there. It was such a silly thing to do. I was basically placing a stone with my name on it on the beach somewhere and waiting for someone to find it.

If you keep doing the same thing over and over again and keep getting the same results just stop. Stop and have a think about what you're doing and more importantly what you're NOT doing. Maybe you know what it is but are too afraid to do it. If you're afraid to do it, chances are that's what you need to do.

Fear is the main thing that needs to be conquered here. It's the hard, intimidating tasks that not many people are prepared to do that will set you apart from others. These are the tasks that separate the wantrepreneurs to the entrepreneurs. The ones that deserve to make money.

Business isn't easy. It's harder then a full-time job no matter how difficult your full-time job may have been. Not because it's more physical. It's more due to the fact that you need to push your mind beyond it's limits of fear and perseverance. Beyond a level 99% of people can't.

You are your own boss. That doesn't mean you can work whenever you want and do little to no work most of the time. That means you are your own _boss._ You have to boss yourself around from time to time. Set yourself straight. Discipline your lazy self and make it work when it doesn't want to. Business isn't the 'easier' option to live life. It's the more fulfilling. You'll still have to work, in mot cases HARDER then you did at your actual job. The difference is that work won't feel like work because you'll enjoy it.

There has been some times I've spent 12 hours+ working and I was so into it all I didn't realise the day had gone. Make me work 12 hours at a job and I'll be counting down every minute after the 8 hour mark.

## 21. Be Patient

Patience is a virtue. We'll all heard that one before but what does it mean and how does it apply to entrepreneurship?

There's a difference between patience and waiting while doing nothing.

Patience is necessary when you need to work through a project and the near is not in sight.

I once had to count 6,000 books and magazine, put them in alphabetical title order and find out the average selling price of each. It was the first proper business venture I put myself in with a friend. It took us 4 weeks of 8 hour work days to get through it all.

The result? We didn't turn a profit in fact, we barely made our money back. I can't recall the actual result but I'm pretty sure we lost money on the whole project.

BUT, I learned a lot about patience and just working through something. Little but consistent tasks are better then one big push every once a week or twice a month. Consistency is what gets results whether it be in the gym or working on your business.

This is the type of patience I'm talking about.

It's easy to want your app idea to top the charts in it's first few days of launch. Maybe even the first few weeks. I'm in a Skype group with someone who launched his idea at the start of 2015. It's 10 months in now and it's starting to make big traction.

Most people would have given up after a few months tops but he didn't. He kept going and now his effort is paying off.

Patience has a lot to do with progress. I don't blame anyone who's been seeing the same results for months and wants to give up. It's hard to continue to motivate yourself when you're putting in all that effort and seeing nothing in return.

This is where small wins are necessary to keep you going. If your idea is worth it and has value, customers should be reflecting this. If you're seeing constructive criticism, strong points that your idea has helped someone in some way, then you're making progress. Whether it's a sale or just some feedback, that's progress. It's another reason why 'hard tasks' are better than 'soft tasks'.

## 22. Balancing Stubbornness with Real World Data

This will touch on a couple of points mentioned above but it's an important point in itself. Stubbornness is sometimes good in entrepreneurship. There will be a bunch of people that will tell you something can't be done and a stubborn but determined person may show them wrong but there's a limit to how stubborn one should be.

Testing an idea is usually the process of putting it out there and seeing what data you get back. By data I'm referring to customer comments, feedback, whether they re-buy or just use it once and never return, they should give you an indication as to where your idea currently stands.

When you run these 'tests', and your data tells you again and again that your idea sucks, it may be time to give it up. Maybe it DOES have potential. Maybe there's something that's missing in the whole equation that you need to fix to flip things around. You may be too inexperienced to identify what needs to be done right now so it might be a better idea to work on another business.

Over time I've realised that time is valuable. If I'm working on something that caps me at making 100k a year, I'll be experimenting with other things that have the potential to make me even more money. I might stumble upon something that I can work on the same amount of time yet it will yield me 300k.

If your business idea has you going around in circles for too long, treat it as a trial business, learn your lessons and move on. No time was wasted, you learned, you realised what works what doesn't, you at least now have ONE business idea out of your head. You've decluttered your mind and have become more focused. There's only better things from this point.

Being true to yourself is the most important thing here.

## 23. The Idea of Focusing on Appeal

Focus is a big part of business. The entrepreneurs who appear on Shark Tank with a great product and have a plan in place how they're going to get this single product into every household in America are the ones that get attention. Sometimes people have great ideas that are making waves but are already thinking of expanding their product range into 100 different types instead of the one.

This MIGHT seem like a good idea but it shows a dint in focus and that's when the investors become concerned. You see, catering for everyone might give you a much broader market to work with BUT it will not allow you to stand out.

If you're going to make another platform just like FaceBook that caters for every persons online social needs, why would people make the switch? Ok cool, you might have some extra features that allow people to do things differently but it still serves the same function right?

Instead of that, why not make a FaceBook type platform but solely for Foodies? You may not get the whole world on it but any food lover that loves cooking and sharing their food creations is going to want to join it and be part of the food lover community. I'm not saying the idea will 100% work, I'm illustrating the difference between a focused idea and an unfocused idea.

I remember when I was making t shirt designs to sell on my platform. I'd make designs that would have generic motivational sayings. Maybe some designs with saying that refer to dog lovers, etc. I saw NO results till I started to make more specific designs.

I'd make shirts that said, 'I'm a Chihuahua Girl in a Chicago World'. The specificness might have stopped a lot of people from buying but because it was so focussed on this particular set of demographics, (Girl, Chihuahua owner, Living in Chicago), they sold like hot cakes!

Every girl in Chicago would tag her friend and say, 'OMG this is for us!', and many would follow through with a purchase.

People want to stand out, they like things that cater to their specific interests. The more specific you are with your product creation and marketing,

the more appeal you'll have to your target
demographic.

## 24. Spending Wisely

I know of someone who, before he even wrote down a business plan wanted to spend $500 on a professional design on his business logo. I mean, seriously? How much of a difference do you think a business logo is going to make on a website when trying to sell merchandise? Especially at the start of a business when there's been 0 branding.

Every business has to start from being a nobody. You have to give that business personality, character, an identity it can only be shaped into by interacting with the world.

Don't spend money on unnecessary things that just make you feel good. Before spending money on a beautifully designed website or logo, spend money on FaceBook advertising, driving traffic to a landing page that pitches your product. See how people react and compare those results with a different landing page with a different product or idea on it.

The best money spent at the start is that which collects data. Data could simply mean information on whether your idea is good or bad.

Peoples email addresses who are interested in learning more about your product or better yet, are interested in buying it.

FaceBook had only ONE goal at the early stages of the company and that was to grow it's user base to a certain amount. Any activity that didn't directly contribute to this idea was scrapped no matter how good of an idea it sounded like.

As an entrepreneur you need to be able to see through the activities that matter very little and those that matter a lot. It's easy to get caught up feeling productive doing activities that contribute very little to you building a business.

At certain points, take a step back and ask yourself whether it's a good idea or not to do what your currently doing. Can this money be better spent. If the answer is yes, then STOP immediately and do what you need to do. I know this is easier said then done but doing what counts at the early stages of your business is crucial to it's success.

## 25. Doing One Task Instead of 10

Another topic on focus. This one is different.

This topic refers to the idea of focus when trying to get work done.

For a long time I was the type of person that would just do any task that would come to mind. I'd be in the middle of that task and something else would pop in and I'd switch to that. I'd keep going around in circles never really finish anything completely, just ending up doing a lot of everything. This was me at work.

My manager who would sit in front of me would do the opposite of this. He'd list the tasks he needed to do and work through them _one by one._ He wouldn't even consider looking at the next task until the current task was 100% finished.

Over the course of a year, I realised he was achieving so much more than me. So much so that I started implementing his method. Even till this day I use the 'one task at a time' approach. I'll close all unrelated browser tasks until that one task is finished and out of the way.

The thing that most people don't realise is that when you keep switching from one task to another, your mind wastes a little bit of time adjusting to the switch. It goes from completely focused to unfocused for a short while till it gets in the groove of things again. Then, just as it's getting used to working on this task, you switch to another, resetting the mental process. You never really give your mind the chance to really start rolling, 100% focused on that task.

I highly recommend this approach over anything else. Tell yourself your not going to touch any social media unless you finish this task. Take a 5 minute break once your done and go on to the next one. You'll achieve a lot more work guaranteed.

## 26. Do the Scary Things First

This one relates to point number 24, (spending wisely).

Business is full of uncertainty. The uncertainty of not knowing whether or not the idea you're working on is a good one. Most people that come from a job background have a hard time dealing with this uncertainty. Jobs have managers that tell you what to do. But in this case, YOU are your own manager and have to come up with your own tasks. What happens when you finish them?

The answer to this depends on the task your doing. It's easy to get caught up doing things you're comfortable with. People with designing jobs will do design work first for their business. Developers will do the development and coding work first, it's only natural.

Rarely do you get someone who will do the hardest tasks first. Tasks that challenge your ability to deal with people. For most people these tasks are 'scary'.

If you're willing to pick up the phone and cold

call 100 people to pitch your business idea, you are already miles ahead of other beginner entrepreneurs.

Same thing with being able to set aside a spending budget and spend it while knowing you're losing money BUT learning.
Being able to make that phone call to the coach/mentor you've had in mind and asking him for advice is another one.

Tasks like the above three are hard to deal with because they test a certain part of you that's insecure. These insecurities are nothing but fears in the unknown. They need to be drilled out of you. Hurdles that need to be jumped over.

Do these tasks first. Whatever your afraid of is keeping you from evolving to the next level as an entrepreneur. The quicker you can jump these hurdles, the quicker you can achieve your goals.

Be fearless in your approach to business. It will take you very VERY far.

## 27. Time is More Valuable Than Money.

I feel like a lone soldier believing in this sometimes. I'm the type of guy that will pay $2 at the atm thats not from my bank to save myself from walking 2 levels and across the other side of the shopping centre to find my banks atm.

Here in Australia they have trollies that require you to put $2 in them to unchain themselves from the other trollies so you can use it. I'll sometimes return it to another trolley stand and sacrifice my $2 because I can't be bothered spending 10 minutes to take it back to the original place.

Time for me, and many other entrepreneurs is more valuable than money. It takes a damn long time to fully understand and apply this concept in business. Especially if you're coming from a 9-5 working background.

I used to be the opposite of the above. I'd go to extra lengths to save a little bit of cash. I'd spend hours on end on small business tasks that I can easily get someone else to do for me. Sure, you can do it yourself for free but you eventually come to a realisation that there's a set of tasks in your business that matter the most. Tasks that directly contribute to the growth of your business.

These tasks are what you should be spending your working hours on. Imagine the below scenario. The %'s refer to how much this task contributes to the growth of your business.

Task A – Paperwork - 10%
Task B – Programming -15%
Task C – Designing - 15%
Task D – Networking – 60%
**TOTAL = 100%**

Now, imagine all these tasks required 2 hours of the working day to complete. You can see by the above percentages that Networking has the biggest contribution towards the growth of your business. If you spent only 1 hour on the first 3 tasks and 4 hours on Networking let's see what the % contribution will now look like.

Task A – Paperwork - 5%
Task B – Programming – 7.5%
Task C – Designing – 7.5%
Task D – Networking - 120%
**TOTAL = 140%**

Your spending the same 8 hours at work, yet your spending more time on what matters.

Let's now pretend we're going to outsource the first 3 tasks at 2 hours a day and you're going to spend the whole 8 hours focusing on networking.

Task A – Paperwork - 10%
Task B – Programming – 15%
Task C – Designing – 15%
Task D – Networking - 240%
**TOTAL = 280%!**

Notice how much more you can achieve? It might cost you some money to outsource these tasks and it's up to you to work out whether or not the growth of your business is worth the outsourcing costs but in most cases, when you figure this formula out for your business, that's when the real magic happens.

Now remember, this is just an example and although the percentages may not be realistic, the comparison to the real world is still applicable.

You only get so many hours in the working day. The reality is, you CAN'T do everything. It's just not possible. You need to work out which tasks require your time and which can be outsourced. Managing and optimising your costs on outsourced work and getting things done quicker is a corner stone to successful businesses. I know it's a hard concept to wrap your head around but the people that do implement this concept are the ones that make it big.

## 28. Importance of Split Testing

Split testing is how a business gets better. It's a process of testing one assumption against another and seeing which gives better results. This can play out in many ways in business.

FaceBook does it all the time when they add new functionalities to their platforms. Upon release or updates you will notice not everyone will receive the updated features, only a select few. FaceBook will then see how these new users are responding. If they respond positively and engagement increases then they'll slowly release it to the rest of the Facebook world. If not, they'll take it out of their platform and write it off as a bad idea.

Most people when starting a business don't understand the concept of split testing. Maybe they just don't think it's an important piece of the puzzle.

Everything in business that has reached a point of profitability was the result of the constant split testing of several ideas. Whether this works better or that. Do people respond to this product more or another one. Do grey shirts better than blue. As you split-test you get closer and closer in building the ideal product for your customers.

At the end of the day, this is what it boils down to.

Split testing can even be the process of implementing your business ideas and seeing which one gives the best results. You may be doing this subconsciously. If your business activities allows you to discard a certain idea or concept, decluttering your mind even the slightest, then you're doing it right.

People in the online space split test like maniacs. From website names to button text, EVERYTHING is split tested. There are softwares out there that will measure where your customers are clicking the most, what page their engaging more in. You can test a page against another and the software will tell you which is performing better.

Business that make decisions off real data they've gained through split testing a variety of things are the one that improve the quickest. They'll be directed along the right way and eventually will create something their customers love. This is how business is done right.

## 29. Eating and Being Mentally Healthy

Business is a lot more then just sitting down doing work or networking with people. It's a lifestyle.
The same way going to the gym and exercising also means you need to be disciplined when eating, being an entrepreneur means you have to take care of your body and mind so you can maximise it's output.

I don't know a single famous entrepreneur who doesn't incorporate health and well being into his daily routine.

Anthony Robins drinks a huge green smoothie in the morning.

My uncle hikes every weekend to challenge his business mind and focus

A lot of entrepreneurs swear by morning meditations and morning runs.

When your winning at everything around you, winning at business will start to happen as well.
Business has taught me a lot about achieving

goals. Any goal can be achieved with the necessary determination and work ethic. Its up to you whether you're willing to do it or not.

If you find yourself staying at home all the time surfing the internet for business ideas, hardly attempting any of them and isolating yourself from healthy food and exercise, your mind will start to lose it's belief in itself.

The brain is like a muscle, it gets stronger with practice. When you learn new ways to do things, your brain grows and changes for the better. This has actually been determined by scientists.

Incorporate healthy habits into your routine. Whether it's something small like a morning jog or a morning smoothie, they all add up and build your mind into something more ready to take on the business world.

## 30. No Time for Girlfriends

A business is a commitment. It's like having a job or playing a professional sport. It will dominate your time, your thoughts, your eating habits, everything you do will be centred around your business. Whether you're in it part-time or full-time at some point the above will happen.

You have to be VERY selective of where else to dedicate your time to.

I thought I'd be more available for my friends and family when I work for myself. In a way I am, but 90% of the time I'm busy with myself.

To be able to put yourself in the right business mindset is half the challenge. It requires a lot of discipline which can be learned outside of business.

I dedicate myself to boxing. I compete to force myself to take it more seriously. I eat VERY healthy so I can fulfil my sports and business goals. These are my priorities right now. If you feel like these are important aspects of your life, don't waste someone else's time being in a relationship.

I'm not one to give personal advice and I thought of leaving this point out but I've seen a trend amongst those that have a partner and those that don't. A partner often requires a lot of time whether they say it or not. Being there for them mentally and physically, having to think about the future, dealing with small issues that put you in a bad mood are all points that confuse your focus. The less you have on your mind the better.

If you're not able to prioritise a relationship right now and business is your main priority then keep it at just that. Go out, meet people, be nice. Be friendly but when you go to your business, you should be able to work on with nothing else in mind.

Some people with a healthy relationship might think this point is irrelevant. Maybe it is for you guys and I'd say your blessed. I've seen some very supportive partners who understand the importance of space and can deal with their partner being busy for long periods of time. This one's not for you guys. Keep doing what your doing. But if this point DOES apply, think of it long and hard and make the necessary decisions to get you to where you want to be.

# Conclusion

You may or may not have heard about the above points but they are realisations that you make as you further your entrepreneurship journey. Most of them can only be realised when you start to take business seriously and prioritise it as one of your top goals.

Remember, you don't have to get everything right at the start. It's more important to make a start then to be paralysed over 'what to start on'.

There is no wrong or right answer in business. Each decision will just lead to more decisions. Business is a messy venture at the start and the only way to make sense of it all is to just jump in and start something.

It's like trying to untangle a tangly mess of wires. The only way to get through it all is to pick a starting point and just get started. It might lead to a dead end but at least you'll know which lead to dead ends and which don't.

There are millions of ways to make a million

dollars and as long as you keep going, learning from every mistake you'll become a better entrepreneur with every passing week.

Give yourself the mental freedom and time to go, just as you would when committing to an educational course of 3-6 years.

Business can be learned by anyone that is willing to look at it realistically.

All the best to whomever decides to take the challenge.

Mateen Soudagar